CLOSE ENCOUNTERS

OF THE LOVING KIND

© The Stanborough Press Ltd., 1992

First published 1992

ISBN 1-873796-07-2

Published by Autumn House Publications
a division of The Stanborough Press.

Printed and bound by
The Stanborough Press Ltd.,
Alma Park, Grantham, Lincs.,
NG31 9SL, England

CONTENTS

PREFACE

Wherever Jesus went, huge crowds of people followed, and where there are huge crowds there are children. *Close Encounters of the Loving Kind* tells the stories of some of the children who could have met Jesus.

The Gospel accounts are brief and to the point, and we are often left wondering, What happened next? (Well I am!) Some of the stories in this book try to answer that question.

It's also fascinating to see the well-known stories through someone else's eyes, for instance, the daughter of the woman at the well. You didn't know she had a daughter? She had five husbands, she must have had a daughter!

Where possible I have tried not to add to Scripture, but just occasionally I've used my imagination to find out what could have happened next, and I've put words into people's mouths which do not appear in the Bible. I wonder if you'll spot them without turning to your New Testament?

What a tremendous experience it must have been to meet Jesus! I had a lot of fun putting myself in the shoes of children aged between 9-14 who could have done just that. I hope you have as much fun reading their very individual stories.
ANITA

THE STAR

by Philip

There wasn't a cloud in the sky that night, and high overhead there were thousands and millions of stars. It was so light that we could easily see the sheep moving about as they settled down for the night.

Later, at the entrance to the pen, leaning against my Dad as we sat by the fire, I listened and watched as he pointed out his favourite groups of stars. But I wasn't really listening. It was late and I'd had an exciting day going to work with Dad.

First he'd shown me how to find good pasture. You see there are many poisonous plants in the grass which a good shepherd must avoid. He'd asked me to check the water drawn from a cistern deep in the hillside, and sent me with a burning stick to clear the ground of snakes while he checked for wolves and jackals. We'd had our work cut out getting the sheep penned in the late afternoon. They each have to be checked, see, for injuries. I held the jar of olive oil and Dad let me rub it on the sheep's legs if he noticed them limping. If they had scratches or cuts he bathed the wound with fresh cedar-tar.

As you can imagine, after all this I was tired and as I sat with him by the fire my head began to feel swimmy, full of sheep and stars, and I didn't need to count either before I was fast asleep.

I woke to hear the voice of Seth, one of Dad's friends. He

sounded a bit excited. 'Have you noticed that big star? It's even brighter on the other side of the hill.'

I felt Dad chuckle softly. 'You left your sheep on their own just to come round here and tell me about a star?'

' 'Course not,' Seth replied. 'Young Jamie's with me tonight. He's shaping up well. The sheep are fine. But look at that star! You're the expert. Which one is it?'

I struggled into a sitting position as Dad shielded his eyes to single out the star, but after a moment he scrambled up onto his knees, knocking me over again. As I got up he was suddenly as excited as Seth. 'I've never seen it before,' he said, 'but I'll tell you one thing, it's *moved* since you pointed it out!' He gazed a little longer, then said more slowly, 'No. Maybe I was wrong. It's not moving now, anyway.'

Suddenly it was as if all the stars lost their grip on the sky and started falling down on our heads. As they fell they got bigger and bigger, and — don't laugh — they seemed to be singing. But not like any singing I'd ever heard before. And then we seemed to be in the middle of a kaleidoscope. The colours were incredible and so strong that you almost felt as if you were *hearing* the colours and *looking* at the singing — they were so mixed up together.

Then one clear voice rang out above all the rest. 'Don't be afraid. I bring you good news of great joy for all people. Today in Bethlehem a Saviour has been born . . . he is Christ the Lord. You'll find the baby . . . lying in a manger.'*

Then, about roof height, thousands, it seemed, of other voices joined in a great chorus as if they couldn't hold back any longer:

'Glory to God in the highest, and on earth peace to all men!'

Slowly, so slowly you didn't realize it was happening, the singing and the kaleidoscope moved away.

Dad quickly threw some more logs on the fire till it filled the entrance to the sheep pen, and grabbed me by the shoulder.

'Come on!' he yelled. 'Follow them!'

As we puffed our way up the rise leading to Bethlehem, I wondered how we'd know which manger, but there was no doubt once we were level with the houses. A cave in the hillside near the edge of the town was just about lit up by the kaleidoscope of colours. The houses were in pitch darkness by comparison.

At the entrance we stopped, out of breath, wondering what to do next. The sound of singing was gentler here, and the lights sort of furry round the edges. But we knew it was the place. Dad pushed open the rough rush matting hanging at the entrance.

Inside a man lay asleep on the floor, his head resting in the crook of his arm, his hand covering his eyes. A manger had been taken off the wall and set down on the floor, and we could just see tiny hands and feet waving about above the edge. A lady, looking tired yet at the same time very happy, was gazing down at the manger and making soft cooing noises.

She looked at us, afraid for a moment, then relaxed when Dad pushed me forward. I suppose he wanted to show her we meant no harm. A proud sort of smile spread over her face. 'Would you like to see the baby?'

Now I'm not much of a one for babies, but this one — well, he was only tiny, and he did look a bit special, but could a baby really save us all? While I was thinking how to ask the lady about this, Dad came up behind me and knelt beside the manger. He looked at the baby for a while, and then at the lady for a long time. Nothing was said but he had a question in his eyes and somehow she managed to answer without a word. Then Dad pulled me down to my knees and as he bowed his head, I heard him murmur: 'Glory — glory to God in the highest.'

As we made our way back to the field, Dad and Seth were very quiet, and so was I. I was wondering what the other shepherds on our hill would say when we told them what we'd seen. Out there in the cold night again it all seemed too wonderful to be true. I thought they'd laugh at us. But they didn't. Great, rough men that they were, they all looked as if they wished they'd been to the manger too. Their eyes went all soft and sort of gentle, and they kept asking us to tell them again what the baby looked like. He was the *real* star, that baby.

---

* See Luke 2.

THE RIVER

by Becca

I'd been a bit worried about Mum and Dad for a while. That is, till the day we all went to the river together. They seemed to have been mad at each other for ages. Till we went to the river together. Hardly a day passed without one of them losing their temper or shouting at the other. They almost seemed to hate each other. Till we went to the river.

They had even started on us kids. It had become so bad that we could hardly open our mouths without getting into trouble. Till that day at the river.

So what's so special about this river? I expect you're asking. I'll tell you.

It all started when Mum came in from the market and said to Dad, 'Everyone's talking about that hermit preacher down by the river.'

'Seven-day wonder,' muttered Dad.

'No', said Mum, taking his words literally, 'he's been baptizing people for weeks.'

'Baptizing people?' Dad asked. 'What for?' His voice had risen and I thought, Oh, no, not again, but Mum said quite gently:

'It's to wash them clean of their sins.'

She paused, then went on: 'Give them a fresh start, I suppose . . . . ' Her voice trailed off, rather wistfully, I thought, and I waited to see what Dad made of it.

'A fresh start', he repeated, almost to himself.

'Mmmmmm,' said Mum, and they went quiet for a while.

After what seemed ages Mum said, in that same wistful voice, '*We* need a fresh start.'

Dad pursed his lips and was quiet for a while, then he stood up suddenly and made for the door. 'Pack a picnic lunch, Leah. We'll take Becca and the baby. I'll be back soon. There's something I've got to finish.'

He paused with his hand on the latch, as if he were about to say something else, then changed his mind and went out.

I looked at Mum. Her eyes were full of tears but she was smiling. She just stood there, looking at the door, then she wiped her eyes on her sleeve and said, 'Fetch the basket then, Becca. You heard what your father said.'

There were crowds and crowds of people at the river. Dad had wandered down to see what was going on. I settled little Joseph on a blanket and was going to see if any of my friends were around, when Mum stopped me. 'Don't wander off, Becca', she said. 'Let's stay together today, eh?'

Sensing it was important to her, I nodded and she gave me a hug. 'I've got a feeling things are on the mend already', she said, and she looked so happy and excited that all I could do was give her a huge hug back.

We had our picnic lunch — it wasn't time for lunch but Joseph and I were starving. Then Dad picked up Joseph and we went right to the river's edge.

A man dressed in a rough, hairy sort of coat was talking to masses of people all sitting on the rocks or standing if they were further away.

'Repent of your sins!' he cried. 'And be baptized. God's kingdom is very near!'*

Someone called out, 'Why do we need to be baptized?'

The preacher said, 'Don't think that just because you were born a Jew you will be allowed into God's kingdom.' Then he repeated what he'd said before, but louder: 'You must repent and be baptized!'

He went down into the river till it was up to his waist and opened his arms to those who had begun to make their way towards him. Someone near him asked: 'Are you the Saviour God promised to send us?'

The Baptist shook his head. 'I am not that Saviour. I baptize with water only. He will baptize with the Holy Spirit of God. Get ready! That Saviour is coming!'

Then for a while he was busy baptizing people. It was clever the way he did it — and so quick. He asked God's blessing on the person, then putting one arm round their shoulders and getting them to hold onto his other arm, he lay them back in the water so that it swirled over them, but only for a second before he was lifting them dripping out of the water.

I looked to see what Dad and Mum were making of it, and saw them looking at each other. Mum nodded to him, then turned to me.

'Take Joseph', she said. Then, taking Dad's hand, she went down to the water with him. I stood on the bank with the baby.

Before they reached the Baptist, though, he had stopped what he was doing and was staring at a man making his way down the bank. It was only when the man walked into the water that the Baptist found his voice again. He didn't shout this time, but his words carried across the water quite clearly.

'No, Master!' he said. 'I need to be baptized by you, and yet you come to me?'

The man said, 'It is good for us to show that we belong to God's kingdom.'

The Baptist didn't argue any more, but placed his arm round the man's shoulders and lowered him into the water.

What happened next was like a beautiful dream. It had been a cloudy day, but at that moment a parting came in the clouds and fantastic beams of light shone down, sparkling the water and making everything golden. Suddenly, just above the man's head, there appeared a shape like a dove. Its wings rose and fell, sending sparks of light all round, like a halo, until it landed on the man's shoulder.

Then an incredible voice said: 'This is my beloved Son in whom I am well pleased.'

I don't know where the voice came from, but it sort of filled your head, if you see what I mean. Afterwards some people said it came from the sky, some said it had thundered, and some said it came from the dove.

I think it was God's voice. I know I'd never heard God speak directly like that before, but if he did, that's exactly how he'd sound.

As the man left the water people started asking each other who he was, and I heard someone say, 'Jesus of Nazareth, the carpenter.'

Then the Baptist called the people to repent again and went back to baptizing. But he looked in a bit of a daze, like you do when you've seen something you just can't believe.

Mum and Dad made their way to him, and Dad stood there while Mum was baptized first. Then she stood while he was baptized. As they came up out of the water hand in hand I ran with Joseph to meet them and we all hugged, even though they were wet through.

Things have been great since then. Mum and Dad are really happy, and so are we. Oh, and we've just heard that Jesus is back in the area so we're all going to hear him speak. People are saying he's not just a great preacher but he might be the Saviour.

Well, if he is God's son, like the voice said, he would be the Saviour, would'nt he?

---

*See Matthew 3.

THE STORM

by Jacob

It had been a long day. Even then, with the sun setting, masses of people were still crowding round Dad and his friends. To be honest, I was getting angry. Dad had promised to let me go fishing with them that night and I'd been sitting in the boat for ages, wishing the crowd of people a million miles away.

It isn't often Dad lets me go with them nowadays, specially since he started going about with the Preacher and his friends. Well, he hasn't done so much fishing. Mind you, I'm not complaining. Dad's been a lot better-tempered lately. I can't remember the last time he threw me out of the boat for making a nuisance of myself. Good job I learned to swim before I could walk!

The ride was a reward for working hard at school. And, boy, had I worked hard! Straight-A-student, that was me! And all for a night's fishing that was getting further and further away!

There was another reason I was getting agitated. If we didn't cast off soon, Mum would be wondering where I was, and if she wandered down to find me there'd be trouble. I hadn't got round to telling her where I was going because she'd got a job lined up for me at home, and if she'd found out I wasn't coming home. . . .

At last! A bit of action. The talking had stopped and Dad and the others were heading towards the boat. I tried to look busy. Wouldn't do for them to see me sitting on a cushion. I tried to look as if I was coiling up a rope.

Then we were on our way. One or two other boats set off with us, but at least they'd the sense to give us a bit of elbow room. The crowd started to head off home.

Dad and the others looked a bit tired when they jumped on board. Not a good start to a hard night's fishing, I thought, but at least Dad was in a good humour. I'm glad I wasn't just a passenger, though, because no sooner had they come on board than Jesus curled up on my cushion! He really looked all in, and I heard Dad say they could manage without him. Fast asleep he was, in seconds. Well, he's not a fisherman so he's not a lot of use in a boat anyway.

It was pitch dark when the storm struck. Dad heard it coming but not soon enough. It hit us with everything it had. The waves were so high they were coming over the side of the boat. Dad threw me a baling pan and ordered those who weren't hanging on to things to grab one as well. After that it was just bale, bale, bale, as if our lives depended on it — which they did! It got very rough! That was the end of that night's fishing! Trust me to pick a night when they got mixed up with a storm.

I began to get angry again, and was baling like mad when I noticed that Jesus was still asleep on that cushion! I couldn't believe it. Chaos breaking loose round his head and he was still fast asleep!

'We could use another hand on the baling!' I yelled to no one in particular, but nobody heard me. I baled faster, but we were gaining water quicker than we could shift it. It annoyed me that Jesus was sleeping like a baby while we were trying to save the boat, so I yelled again about the baling. Dad heard me that time and saw me point to Jesus. Then, still hanging on to the sail which had been only half down when the storm struck, he inched his way over.

'Teacher!' I heard him shout. 'Don't you care if we drown?'*

Now you're not going to believe what I'm going to tell you next, but it's as true as I was standing there baling for my life.

Jesus woke up, got to his feet, and said: 'Quiet! Be still!'

For a second I thought he was talking to Dad, but suddenly everything went dead calm. I mean the *sea*, and the *wind!*

For another second no one moved. Just stood there looking absolutely terrified, which was funny really because they hadn't looked terrified while the boat had been sinking! (Probably because they hadn't time, come to think of it.)

Jesus looked a bit baffled. 'Why are you so afraid?' he asked. 'Do you still have no faith?'

Somewhere at the other end of the boat I heard someone say, 'Who *is* this? Even the wind and waves obey him!'

Jesus heard them too, and looked even more baffled.

'What did you expect me to do?' he asked.

No one answered. Then Dad, speechless for once, snatched the baling pan from me, and held it out to him.

For a moment no one spoke or moved, and then Jesus started to laugh. I'll never forget that laugh. It was as if someone had told him a huge joke and he had found it a real rib-tickler. Then Dad saw the funny side, and his great guffawing laugh made me laugh too. It always does. And before long everyone was sitting down or rolling about, laughing fit to bust.

Did I really say Jesus wouldn't be any use in a boat?

---

*See Mark 4:35-41.

LITTLE BROTHER

by Lydia

I was just going over to Miriam's house to have a look at her new dress when Mum shouted from the kitchen. I pulled a face but tried to make my voice sound pleasant. 'What's up, Mum?'

'If you're going out take Moshe with you.'

'Oh, Mum', I pleaded, 'Must I? We'll be talking girl-talk and you know what a pest he . . . '

She appeared suddenly in the doorway, holding the pest by one hand. The look on her face said I'd be in trouble if I didn't do as I was told, so I pulled another face and took his grubby little hand.

'All right, come on then. But if you do what you did last time I'll . . . '

'Lydia!'

'It's OK, Mum. I'll look after him.'

'And no bullying!'

As if I would! I just try to make sure he does as he's told. But, honest, he really is a pain. He's always breaking things and spoiling my clothes and generally getting in the way. And he's not that little really, he's nearly 6 and I think he should be learning a bit more sense by now.

And as I expected, he started the minute we reached Miriam's.

'I want to go play with Benny.'

Benny was the little boy next door but Mum's told me not   *19* to let Moshe play with him because he's very rough and the two of them are a force to be reckoned with.

So I hauled him yelling up the outside stairway at Miriam's and up onto the roof where we kids spend most of our time. You wouldn't believe the names he called me, but Miriam found a little trolley for him to fill with peas and he settled down. Benny was nowhere to be seen anyway, so that helped.

Once he was busy, Miriam whispered, 'Are you coming inside to see my dress, then?'

I looked at Moshe. 'Will you be good and stay up here?'

He nodded, not taking his eyes off the peas he was loading, and Miriam and I went down.

We were down there quite a bit because we're the same size, more or less, and she let me try the dress on. It was in that lovely soft, floaty sort of material, deep blue with thin golden threads woven into the pattern, and it made me look at least two years older. Definitely not the sort of dress I'd be able to persuade Mum to let me have!

Then I remembered Moshe. 'We'd better get back up on the roof', I said. 'You just can't trust him.'

Sure enough, as we came up the stairs I could see, as my head topped roof-level, that there was no sign of Moshe.

'That does it', I told Miriam as she checked behind some boxes in case he was hiding. 'This time he's in real trouble when I find him.'

'If you find him, you mean?' she said helpfully, but I was already halfway down the stairs.

'I know exactly where he'll be', I yelled back. 'He wanted me to take him to see the fishing boats.'

I stopped. 'Miriam, will you stay here and keep an eye open for him. If he comes — hang on to him. You have my full permission to start beating him if you like! If I don't find him by the sea I'll come straight back, then I'll take over!'

I shot off towards the shore.

Oh, no, I thought as I got nearer. There were masses of

people all round the boats. I'd never find him among that lot! I began skirting round the edge of the crowd, getting angrier and angrier as time went by and there was no sign of him.

In the end I had to pluck up my courage and plough straight into them, elbowing them aside when they ignored me. It's a good job I'm tall for my age or I'd never have got through.

Then I saw him.

I was just about to run over and grab him when it went quiet like it does all of a sudden when a lot of people are talking, and one of the men standing nearby said to another man, 'Jesus, who is the greatest in the kingdom of heaven?'*

Everyone looked at the man he had spoken to. He smiled and began to look around. Spotting Moshe he called him over. Moshe didn't even hesitate. I think he must have seen me heading his way!

The man called Jesus lifted him into the centre of the circle that had formed round them, and said: 'The truth is, unless you change and become as trusting as this little child you won't enter the kingdom of heaven.'

Moshe beamed up at him with his grubby little face and I could have sunk into the ground. Jesus knelt down and put his arm round Moshe as he continued to speak. 'Whoever humbles himself like a child shall be the greatest in the kingdom of heaven. And anyone who hurts one of these little ones would be better off being thrown into the sea with a millstone round his neck.'

I felt a bit uncomfortable then, in view of what I'd been planning to do to our Moshe, but the man had such a nice voice that I wanted to hear what else he had to say — if he got off the subject of little kids, that is! And he did. I couldn't get Moshe back for the time being, and he was safe anyway, so I settled down with the other people who had been sitting down while Jesus talked.

We must have listened to him for ages. He talked about all sorts of things. Like a shepherd searching for a lost sheep, 21 and he put in a bit about his Father not wanting any of his 'little ones' to be lost.

Then it was as if he was talking straight at me, though I don't think he knew I was Moshe's sister. He said: 'If your brother does something against you, discuss the matter with him. Don't make an enemy of him.'

Moshe looked at me then and grinned, as if to say he knew he really was quite safe with that Jesus as his friend!

Then one of the men nearest to them asked Jesus a question. He said, 'Master, how often must I forgive my brother if he does something against me? Would seven times be enough?'

Jesus laughed. 'No, Peter! Seventy times seven would be more like it!'

The man called Peter looked a bit shocked, and Jesus explained more seriously: 'As often as you want your Father in heaven to forgive you.'

Peter puffed out his cheeks as if that was a bit of a tall order, and I must admit, I did the same. Then Jesus, resting his hand on Moshe's head, blessed him. It was a lovely prayer. Moshe closed his eyes, and as he stood there I could see quite clearly the tear-tracks down his face. He must have been crying up on the roof when I went downstairs with Miriam. Daft little kid. Then I remembered what a nasty moment he'd given me, finding him gone from the roof, and I decided I'd give him a rough time anyway because he had to learn to do as he was told. Anything could have happened to . . .

Suddenly I realized that Jesus was looking straight at me. He hadn't finished praying but his eyes were open. 'And let this child find forgiveness, Father, for his little sins. Amen.'

Then, still keeping his eyes on me, he pushed Moshe gently towards me and smiled. Well, I couldn't do anything else. I had to forgive him, didn't I? Specially with Jesus looking at me like that!

Funny thing is, since then I've tried to do what Jesus said, and forgive Moshe when he does anything against me. Now you won't believe me, but we're getting on ever so much better nowadays. At first I thought that if I forgave him he'd play me up even more, but he's not half the pest he used to be, honest, and even when he is, every now and then, I just try to remember the way Jesus looked at me, and it's almost easy forgiving him yet again.

Even Mum's noticed things have been a bit different since Jesus blessed our Moshe. Naturally he told her all about it, with him in the starring role and all!

---

*See Matthew 18:1-35.

THE DIARY

by James

Dear Diary,
Went to a party today and was having a really great time. Won
two of the games and didn't make myself sick though there was
masses of smashing food! We were sitting about, eating, chatting
and laughing, when I felt the evil one coming into my head.
That put a stop to the good time. All the kids were scared out
of their wits, and I wasn't feeling too good when I came to.
I'd fallen onto the fire and burned my arm. When I came round
everyone avoided looking at me. Don't blame them. I must've
looked awful, screaming and foaming at the mouth. Felt very
tired and fell asleep despite the awful pain in my arm. When
I woke up it was night. Another great day ruined.

Dear Diary,
It was Mark's birthday today and he had a party. I wasn't
invited. Don't suppose they've forgotten what happened two
weeks ago. Mum baked me some special things for tea but it
wasn't the same.

Dear Diary,
A terrible day today. The evil one took over again and caused
a bad accident with a lady carrying a baby. She had hysterics
at the sight of me and let the baby drop to the ground. Think
his leg is broken. Poor little thing. Don't know who was

screaming loudest, the baby, the woman or me! But it wasn't funny. Mum's been getting hints that I should be put away. It's not fair, though. I'm OK quite a bit of the time. It's just when the evil one takes over I lose control. If only I knew when it was going to happen I could get out of people's way. . . .

Dear Diary,
My friend was beaten up on the way home from school today because someone called me names and he stuck up for me. It's no good me trying to go any more because the teacher puts me outside the door so that no one is hurt if I get dangerous, and I can't hear very well out there. I miss most of what's going on. Think I'll ask Dad if I can stay at home.

Dear Diary,
Dad let me stay home, but it's worse than being at school. There's nothing to do. Kept getting under Mum's feet until she shouted at me to go outside and play. But when I got outside the evil one came into my head and I rolled all over the clean washing and she had to do it again. She thought I'd done it on purpose to get back at her, but I hadn't, honest. She cried a lot when Dad came home because she was so tired looking after me all day, and not getting a break.

Dear Diary,
Dad says I might have to be locked up. The people round here say I'm too dangerous to have around loose. I suppose I have shot up since my last birthday. I'm nearly as tall as Dad now. He's going to see someone about it tomorrow.

Dear Diary,
Dad looked terrible when he came home, and I soon found out why. He's got to put me away. He explained that it's to keep me safe because people are beginning to threaten what will happen if I hurt any more of their kids. When he described

what it was like, I felt as terrible as he looked! There's all sorts of mad people there, and they do awful things to each other. There's no lessons and I'll never learn anything, just sit there, staring at four walls.

Dear Diary,
Dad's taking me to the 'home' tomorrow. He said they'll visit me often, but what do I do the rest of the time?

Dear Diary,
Today is the worst day of my life. I want to die.

Dear Diary,
Dad came today and said there's a man who might be able to help me. He's a wandering preacher. Dad says if I can just hang on until the next time he's in our village he might get rid of the evil one. . . .

Dear Diary,
Dad came early to get me cleaned up ready to meet the Preacher. Jesus, his name is. Not knowing what he looked like, Dad took me to one of his friends first, but they couldn't do anything. Suddenly this Jesus arrived and everyone crowded round. As soon as I saw him what I'd been dreading happened. The evil one went mad and I followed, went berserk, screaming, throwing myself about, lashing out at everyone and everything, foaming at the mouth . . . . Suddenly I heard a voice. I can't usually hear people when the evil one is in control, but this voice cut like a knife through the racket the evil one was making. And I could see the Preacher standing right in front of me with his hand raised in the air, looking straight at me with the most piercing look I've ever seen.

The evil one didn't like that one little bit because he knew the Preacher was talking to him — not me. Funny, I realized too, that Jesus was looking into me but seeing someone else.

It was as if I was just a spectator. I heard him say very loudly and firmly, 'You! Spirit! I command you to come out of him. And never enter him again!'* Some marching order! But the evil one wasn't going without a fight. He shrieked like a hundred souls in torment and began to throw me about as if I were a rat in the mouth of a dog.

Then I was lying on the ground and someone was saying, 'He's dead.' I realized he was talking about me, and expected to feel as if all the devils in the world had trampled me underfoot. But I didn't. I opened my eyes. I felt great.

The Preacher took my hand and lifted me to my feet. I felt fantastic — ten feet tall. The Preacher was looking at *me* now, not the evil one. We looked at each other for a long time. There wasn't a word big enough to say what I felt, but I knew he'd got the message. He smiled, a deep, friendly smile, all sort of pleased and excited. Then he let go of my hand and went indoors after his friends.

Dad absolutely stared at me. I don't think he could believe it was all over. But I knew it was. Never in my life have I felt so clean and so — whole. There's no doubt the evil one has gone, but I'm glad Jesus told him never to take me over again.

TODAY IS THE FIRST DAY OF THE REST OF MY LIFE AND NOTHING — BUT *NOTHING* — IS GOING TO RUIN THINGS EVER AGAIN!

THANKS, JESUS!

---

* See Mark 9:17-27.

MY MUM

by Davina

My mum can be so embarrassing! Even Uncle James thinks so.

Mum was a bit upset when I refused to call him Dad, but he's *not* my dad. Mum was married to my father around the time I was born but there have been two other 'dads' since then, and now there's Uncle James. Oh, he's all right, in a vague sort of way. He even makes an effort to be a proper dad to us — especially us girls — but he's not my dad and that's all there is to it.

They haven't got married yet so Uncle James doesn't notice some of the more embarrassing things my mum does, like wearing far too much make-up and braiding her hair like a young girl, but even *he* fairly cringes when she gets excited and shrieks with laughing.

I'll say this for Mum, though, she's a jolly sort. Mind you, you have to watch out. One minute she's all smiles and laughing, and the next she's brought the back of her hand across your face so hard you can hardly see afterwards. She's always sorry, though, and the next minute she's all over you, giving you sweets and asking you to forgive her. That can be worse than the slap in the face, believe me, specially if friends are around!

But the other day was the limit. She'd gone off to town for some water — around noon, would you believe! Why she can't go to the well when the other women go I don't know. Or maybe I do. I think they get a bit catty with her, actually. And despite everything she can be quite sensitive at times.

Anyway, she'd been gone ages longer than was necessary and then she comes racing into the house all hot and sweaty, hardly able to breathe (well, she's not as young as she once was), and you won't believe this — *without* the water she went specifically to fetch!

'What's up, Mum?' I asked.

'There's a man', she gasped. Tell me news. Where my mother's concerned there's always a man. My face must have reflected what I was thinking but instead of slapping it she just gasped: 'No. This one is different.'

Pushing my luck I raised a sarcastic eyebrow. She still didn't hit me! This man *must* be different — if only for the effect he's had on her violent streak so far!

'He told me everything I've ever done!'*

My other eyebrow shot up, but she didn't seem to notice, just went rambling on.

'He knew how many husbands I've had', she gasped, 'even that I'm not actually married to Uncle James . . . '

Some man, I thought, but asked: 'Is that all? Maybe he's heard the gossip?'

Then I knew something earth-shattering had happened. That remark had really begged for a slap in the face. But she had suddenly gone all soft at the edges.

'He asked me — me, mind you — for a drink. And he's a *Jew!*'

Oh no, I thought. It's bad enough when Mum's fellers are Samaritans, but if she takes up with a Jew we'll be run out of our solidly Samaritan town in no time. Her next remark was even more unbelievable.

'He told me that if I'd known who it was who asked me for water I would have asked *him* for a drink and he'd have given me living water. Then he told me he's the Messiah. The one we've all been waiting for. God's anointed!'

I'll say this for Mum, despite her life-style she's always

been a great one for religion. But Mum meeting the Messiah?

She sat down suddenly. 'It's true', she said slowly, seeing the disbelief all over my face I suppose. 'I've never heard anyone talk with such authority about the things of God. He said the time is coming when we'll worship the Father not on this mountain nor in Jerusalem, but true worshippers will worship in spirit and truth. And when he said 'the Father' I could see by his eyes and voice he was talking about God as if he were his personal father.'

She looked at me. 'The special way you talk about *your* dad', she explained, and I knew exactly what she meant. Heaven knows, I've annoyed her often enough by doing it.

'When I mentioned the Messiah', she went on, 'he just said "I am he." No fuss, just a simple statement of fact.'

Her eyes filled with tears then (which was a bit off-putting, if you know what I mean), and she stood up suddenly. 'I'm sure he really is the Messiah. I must tell people.'

With that she was gone — rushing out of the house without even fixing her make-up. As I said, my mum can be so embarrassing. And I just knew they'd laugh at her. But the funny thing is that they didn't. People actually believed her. Well, half-believed her. Anyway, they believed her enough to invite a hated Jew to stay in the village for a few days.

Now he's got other people — men as well — believing him. I heard one the other day telling Mum, 'We no longer believe just because of what you said. Now we've heard for ourselves and we know this man really is the Saviour of the world.'

Things are different in our house now. For a start — not being able to do anything about her previous husbands, who've all remarried, Mum decided her relationship with Uncle James had to be put right and they're getting married tomorrow. But that's just a formality. I heard her promise the day before Jesus left that there'd be no other men for her now. Uncle James was it. She'd love him and be faithful to him for ever. And she admitted she'd never said that before! We'll really be a proper family then. In fact we are already. Things are so much better. Mum's toned down the make-up and is dressing more her age. She's gentler and hasn't hit any of us since Jesus came to stay.

There's only one snag. Now she's always kissing us and making a fuss of us in front of our friends, so she can still be very embarrassing to live with. But I wouldn't change her for the world. And to think it's happened all because a Stranger told her all she'd ever done — and didn't reject her for it!

---

*See John 4.

THE BLESSING

by David

I'd had it with Dad. I was sick of looking after two horrible kid brothers and one stupid kid sister! He expected me to drop everything I wanted to do and look after them just because I'm the oldest.

At first when Mum died everyone came round and we had so many offers of help we didn't have to do anything. But after a few weeks people weren't so eager, and now they walk the other way when they see us coming. No kidding! Take Joseph's mum. She was in our house every day until about three weeks ago. Yesterday she dashed into the bakery when she clapped eyes on me taking Sara for a walk. Sara noticed it too. She started to pull me faster towards Joseph's mum, but when she vanished into the bakery Sara pulled a face and stopped tugging.

'Joseph's mum doesn't like us anymore', she said. I told her she did but that she was probably busy.

'No', said Sara, 'she hasn't been to our house at all for weeks.'

I couldn't argue with that so I shut up and bought her a corn dolly to take her mind off it because she looked really down in the dumps and that's not like her. She can be a pain sometimes, but she's usually a jolly little kid.

It's not been easy for her — Sara, that is — since Mum died. In fact I think she's been hit the hardest. As long as the other two have each other they're fine. Oh, they were upset at first, crying and asking Dad why it had to happen to us. But they seem to be getting over it now, and as I said, they're inseparable — where you see one of them you see the other.

Me, I've always been a bit of a loner. Except for Dad. There was a time I'd have done anything for him. But he's gone too far now. I never see him, and on the rare occasions he looks for me, it's to tell me to do something or look after some kid 'properly'. But it's not fair. I was going to start my apprenticeship with the carpenter next week. Now Dad says I'll have to wait, he needs me at home. What sort of life is that for his first-born son? If I leave it too late to start my apprenticeship the carpenter will find someone else.

It's not *just* that. We used to go everywhere together, fishing, rock-climbing, or just walking in the hills. He used to come into the yard and say, 'Get your sandals on, my lad', and off we'd go. Usually early in the morning before he started work. I'm one of nature's early-risers just like Dad. The others weren't usually up and Sara is too young, so nobody minded when we went off together.

But that's all changed now, and I've had enough. I've been asking Dad to find someone to look after us, but he just goes all quiet and moody on me. When I went on about it the other day he shouted at me, but I wasn't prepared to let it go at that and tackled him again last evening. I'd decided it was now or never.

At first he told me to shut up about it. Then when I continued as if he hadn't spoken he went mad and grabbed the carpet beater and started laying into me. I still wouldn't let up, though, shouting and even swearing at him, and in the end he locked me in the cellar for the night.

He sent Simon to let me out this morning, with a message that he was sorry and that I could take it easy today, but that's it!

I left Sara with the others, threatening what would happen to them if they didn't look after her properly, and went off down to the lake. Last night gave me plenty of time to think. It's not easy getting to sleep on a cold stone floor when you hurt in places you didn't even know you had places! So I'd made up my mind.

I was going to get a job with one of the fishing boats. Dad would have to get someone to look after the others then. Anyway, it was his problem after last night. Whatever there had been between us he finished off with that carpet beater!

I was going along by the river not far from the village when I saw a huge crowd. Wondering what was going on, I made my way over. A wandering preacher was talking to the crowd about marriage vows or something. Anyway, he was talking about men divorcing their wives when some women pushed forward carrying their babies. There were lots of little kids with them, and I heard one woman say to one of the men: 'We want the Teacher to bless the children before he goes.'

The man looked a bit frazzled at all those kids. 'Not now', he said. 'Can't you see he's busy!'

She wasn't ready to give up, though, and started to go past him. Two or three other women went with her. 'It's not a good time', he said, louder. 'Come back another day. You can't see him now.'

At that moment the Teacher stopped what he was saying and stood up. Walking towards where the women were turning to argue with the man, he looked quite angry, taking hold of the man's arm and moving him aside.

'Let the children come to me, and don't stop them. For of such is the kingdom of God!'*

The man looked embarrassed and started to explain: 'But, Jesus, Master . . . '

Jesus shook his head. 'Honestly, I tell you, whoever will not receive the kingdom of God like a little child, he shall not go there!'

Then he took one of the babies and sat down on a rock. Another baby was laid across his lap, and he put his left arm round the shoulders of a boy who was pushed forward by his mother, drawing him into the circle that had formed round him.

After looking at the mums with a smile, he began to bless the babies and children. It took quite a while, but once he started to pray over them all the tension went. Everyone relaxed and as the mums and some dads took their children back they were all smiles. Even kids who hadn't been too keen on going forward ran back to their mums with smiles on their faces. The man who had told the women to go away got busy again, organizing it so that the children who had been blessed made room for others to come forward. I saw Jesus smile at him so I knew everything was all right between them.

It was then that I thought about Dad. He used to smile at me like that. Before Mum died. And I looked at all those mums, eager for their children to be blessed, and thought about my Mum. She'd wanted the best for us. That's why she'd spoken to the carpenter about my apprenticeship herself — after she'd discussed it with Dad, of course.

Now I'd decided to throw it all away. Or thought I had.

I looked again at the man Jesus and suddenly he caught my eye. He didn't say anything. Just sat there with his hand resting on a little girl's head. But he looked straight at me, just like my Dad used to when we didn't need words to know what the other was thinking. And I remembered how we'd cried together when Mum died, and I realized that just like everyone else I hadn't been much help to Dad either, lately.

As I looked at Jesus he smiled, and I may be mistaken, but he seemed to nod to me slightly before carrying on blessing the other children.

Then I knew what I had to do. Fishing wasn't for me, except with my Dad first thing in the morning. Right now I had to find him and tell him everything would be all right. We'd work things out — *together*, like we'd always done.

I gave Jesus a wave, and started to run home as fast as I could.

THE BURDEN

by Thol

I've got this friend Shimon. He's a lot older than me, and he used to have a wife, but she left him. She took their baby boy with her when she went, and I got the feeling that in some way I helped him get over the loss of his son. I don't know. Anyway, my Dad said it was good that *somebody* was prepared to be his friend.

When I asked him what he meant he said, 'I'll tell you when you get a bit older, Thol.' (Thol is short for Bartholomew, by the way.)

I was a bit put out and reminded him that I'm 13 so according to our tradition I'm already a man.

'True, son,' he said, 'but there are things a young man like yourself is too young to understand.'

I had to leave it at that, but Dad said it was OK to be friends with Shimon, so I was.

He was quite a character too, before his wife and baby left. All the fun seemed to go out of him then, and he was always telling me he wished he hadn't done it. But when I asked him what he wished he hadn't done, he just said, '*God* knows. That's more than enough.'

He used to take me fishing and would let me ride on his great plough horse. It was absolutely enormous but as gentle as a kitten. In return I'd help him pick the stones out of his field and we always shared the fish we caught. He was a great runner too, and we used to race each other. He showed me the right way to run and I got a lot faster after that.

But that was before he became paralysed. People had been avoiding him ever since his wife left, but when he became paralysed it was even worse. Often when I turned up I was the only person he'd seen all day. When I was going on once about people not caring, he just said, 'I don't blame them. I brought this lot on myself. They know it's my fault. It makes them uneasy, being with me. You see, there's nothing they can do. People hate feeling helpless so they stay away.'

I didn't know what to say to that, but I couldn't help wondering what he'd done, though I didn't like to ask. He obviously felt guilty about something. What it could possibly have to do with his paralysis I don't know, but it was none of my business (as my Dad kept telling me!) so I left it. It didn't stop me being his friend. He'd been a good one to me when he was OK, so now it was my turn. He certainly needed a friend.

I used to visit him every day. Sometimes I read to him, or just told him what I'd been doing at school or wherever. He must have liked my visits because he always asked me to come again — tomorrow — and I could tell he meant it. Some days, though, he was so miserable he asked me to leave him alone. I suppose that was because he was visibly getting worse week by week. The doctors couldn't do anything, and the worse it got the more often he asked me to leave him alone. But even on his worse days he always made me promise to keep coming.

I worried about him when I wasn't there. I knew he paid the lady next door to look after him, but he couldn't afford much so it was a bit basic. When I went round to see him I used to tidy things up and make sure he had a drink at least. Sometimes when he didn't want to talk that was what I did instead of just pushing off.

Then one day when I went round to see him he seemed excited about something. Though he was very weak by then, his
eyes were all lit up and he said as soon as I got in the door:

'Thol! Am I glad to see you! I want you to help me get to Peter's house. You know, the biggish house on the corner with the covered-in courtyard.'

I nodded, but wasn't sure how to go about doing what he asked. Before I could say anything he went on: 'Will you go and see Josh and ask if he and Ben will carry me over there right away? Tell him I'll never ask them a favour again if they'll just do this one thing for me.'

Actually, Josh and Ben were quite willing. It's true what Shimon said. They kept away because they couldn't bear not being able to help their friend. If only they'd just gone to see him they'd soon have realized he didn't want a lot doing, he just wanted to know someone cared.

We were quite a cheerful party, joking and laughing, by the time we got him onto a pallet and started carrying him down the street. People stared a bit, but we didn't mind. Shimon had said, just before we left: 'I've heard this Jesus not only heals people but he can forgive sins as well. I don't care if he doesn't heal me, as long as he forgives me! I don't think I can live with this guilt any longer.'

I was still no wiser about this guilt-trip he was on, but I'd be happy just to see him on his feet again. So I did what I could to steady him on the pallet as we trundled off to Peter's house.

When we arrived there were masses and masses of people crowding round, looking in windows, crammed in the door-ways. Ben and Josh lowered the pallet and scratched their heads, not knowing what to do next. They tried asking people to move aside, but no one moved. They were all too intent on hearing what the man inside was saying. We all stood around Shimon, looking a bit stumped. Then suddenly he pointed.

'The courtyard roof!' he yelled. 'It's only rushes and clay. We could make a small hole (you won't mind fixing it after-wards, will you?), then you could lower me in. *Throw* me in, if you like. I'm past caring. Just get me in there!'

Well, Josh looked at Ben, and Ben looked at Josh. Then they both shrugged and picked up the pallet together. It wasn't easy keeping Shimon on the pallet as we made our way up the stone steps. They were narrow and I couldn't go alongside. Anyway, we made it, and rested him on the main roof till we got our breath back. Then we started on the courtyard roof. It came away quite easily. Like Shimon said, it was just rushes and clay, but it made a lovely cool patch in the courtyard below.

As we broke through, the sun shone down on the people below, and our shadows flickered across their heads — which were being showered with bits of clay! The man who was speaking — Jesus, I suppose — looked up suddenly. Ben grabbed his end of the pallet.

'Quick, Josh,' he said, then spoke to the men below. 'Give us a hand, will you?'

Clay and dust were really flying everywhere by then, and people were sneezing and coughing, but someone brought a couple of chairs and by standing on them the men below were able to take the pallet and lower it to the ground at the feet of one very surprised preacher!

He looked highly amused and gave a deep chuckle as he looked up at Josh, Ben and me. We didn't want to miss what happened next so we just lay there on the roof, looking in. Do it, preacher, I said to myself over and over again. Do what he wants. PLEASE.

Then Jesus looked at Shimon. Serious now. He looked for a long time, then said: 'My son, your sins are forgiven.'*

Shimon looked as if he couldn't believe his ears, and I must admit, there were gasps all round. We'd all expected him to say that he was going to heal Shimon, yet at the same time, we knew what he was after was forgiveness. But how did the preacher know?

Anyway, before anything happened we heard someone say, 'That's blasphemy! No one can forgive sins but God!'

A lot of them agreed with the man because they started

nodding and muttering to each other. But Jesus wasn't put out.

'What are you arguing about?' he asked them. 'Which is easier — to say to this man "Your sins are forgiven", or "Get up, pick up your bed and walk"? But, so that you will know that I have power on earth to forgive sins, I'll say it.'

Then, turning back to Shimon, he said, 'Get up, pick up your bed and go home.'

For a moment Shimon just stared at him, but then he started to shake — well, more sort of jerk, really, waving his arms and legs about as if he needed to try them out first.

Next thing he was on his feet and heading for the door through the parting made by people standing there with their mouths hanging open. Funny thing is, he did exactly what Jesus told him to do. He picked up his bed first!

*See Luke 5:18-26.

BACK TO LIFE

by Rhoda

I was with Mum in the market square, waiting while she talked to a friend, when I began to feel ill. Well, not ill exactly, more yukky than anything. I'd go all cold and feel as if all my energy was draining out of my toes. Then it would go and I'd just feel very tired. After this had happened a few times I shuffled a bit to let Mum know I wanted to be off home. She nodded and patted my arm but didn't stop talking. When I began to feel sick and shaky I thought I'd better get her moving in case I fainted or anything embarrassing like that.

At first she was a bit annoyed. 'It's all right for you to talk to your friends all day, isn't it?' she asked, 'But I get out of the house for a few minutes and you can't wait while *I* talk to a friend.' She turned and looked at me to show that although she wasn't shouting or anything, she meant it. And I saw her expression change. I must have looked pale or something.

'You look terrible!' she cried. 'Why didn't you tell me you felt ill?'

'I didn't want you to fuss', I said. My mum is one of the great fussers of the world, and the square was full of boys. Well, there were two over by the pottery, sniggering together over something that probably wasn't even remotely funny. I didn't want them sniggering over me too.

When we reached home Mum made me lie down on the couch and then she put a wet cloth on my forehead. 'You've probably just been out in the sun too long', she said, but I could tell she was worried. I was boiling hot by then and would have been glad to feel a bit chilly again.

She brought me a cup of cold water and I could have poured it all over my face. I was too thirsty, though, so I drained it in one go and just let some of the second lot dribble down my neck instead.

I don't remember much about the next few days except once when I woke up and found Dad staring down at me with a very worried look on his face. I could smell baking so I was surprised to see Dad there at that time of morning. He's a busy man, and the leader of the local synagogue (church). We're lucky if we see him at tea-time usually.

He bent and touched my forehead, twisting his mouth as if trying to make up his mind about something, then said: 'I'm going to fetch someone who might be able to help. You just rest. Dad won't let anything happen to his little girl.'

I lay back on the couch thinking it was funny he should call me his little girl when I'm 12. I tried to get my head comfortable but it was all hot and prickly and pounding like mad, and the room kept going round and round. I could hear Mum thumping dough on the table, and she asked me if I wanted anything but I felt too ill to answer. I lay and listened to my breathing, which sounded a bit loud, until suddenly I realized it had gone quiet. Then I fell into the deepest sleep I've ever had. It was *total* sleep, if you know what I mean. No dreams, nothing, and the next thing you know you're being woken by something. I was woken by the sound of a man's voice.

'Little girl, get up!'* That 'little girl' bit again. I felt someone holding my hand, lifting it up, urging me to follow. I opened my eyes and looked straight into the face of the most handsome man I have ever seen. Actually, I'd never seen him before, and no man had ever touched me before, but I wasn't even embarrassed, which is strange because I usually go bright red if any man but Dad even *speaks* to me.

Before I had time to work out who he might be, or why he was helping me up off the couch, he spoke again, and his voice was so kind, even kinder than Dad's.

'Give her something to eat', he told Mum. And Mum, who had been standing there looking as if she'd just seen a ghost, shot over to the table. Her hands were shaking as she put the little honey cake in my hand. My free hand, that is. I was still hanging onto the man's hand with the other. I felt great and wondered what had happened to the fever. My skin felt lovely and cool, just like the man's hand. Dad spoke.

'This is Jesus', he said. 'He's given you back to us.'

I thought that was an odd thing to say, and Dad looked awkward for a moment as if he was trying to find words to tell me something. 'You know, you'd — you were very ill', he stammered, 'in fact you'd — the mourning women were here by the time we got back.' Even odder, I thought. Mourning women came when someone died! I looked more closely into the man's eyes.

'You brought me back to life?'

He smiled. 'Don't let it worry you', he said. 'There's no doubt you were in a very deep sleep.'

Then, letting go of my hand, he drew my parents aside. 'Best not to tell anyone . . . ', I heard him saying quietly, till Dad burst out, 'But she was — '

Jesus held up a finger then, and put an arm round Dad's shoulder, drawing him away into the far corner of the room, where they murmured together for a while.

Then Mum, crying and laughing at the same time, gave me a huge hug. 'Our own girl', she cried over and over again. 'Our own little girl, back with us. Praise the Lord! Praise his wonderful name.'

They've been playing it down ever since, of course, but I think Dad was right. Jesus *did* bring me back to life. You see, I can remember the sound of my breathing stopping suddenly and then just drifting with no pain or anything — and my head had been *agony*. But I'm glad Jesus didn't go telling everyone. I feel a big enough freak as it is with him and his three friends (Peter, James and John Mum says their names were) all piling into our house like that.

All my friends are making a big thing of that, of course, but if they guessed what *really* happened my life wouldn't be worth living. Even the new life that Jesus gave me.

---

*See Luke 8:40-56.

TEMPLE BOY

by Theo

There's synagogues, see, and then there's the Temple. The synagogue is like your local church, but the Temple is where God's Spirit lives and where the sacrifices are carried out so that sins can be forgiven.

Well, I'm what's called a Temple boy. This means that my parents dedicated me to the Temple when I was a baby and since I was a kid I've lived there, learning everything I can learn about the Law and the prophecies of God.

And it's hard work, I can tell you. Though there are some tremendous teachers (rabbis, we call them), who do their best to make things easier. They teach us in rhymes so that we can remember complicated laws or sayings. And we have parts of the law written on little scrolls tied to our foreheads or wrists. That way we're reminded of them whenever we touch the little leather pouches.

Because I've never known any other way of life I've always been very happy there. People sometimes ask me if I miss my family, but to be honest, the rabbis and other Temple boys are my family. And it's not *all* hard work. We have some great times. And we're allowed to be just kids sometimes, if you see what I mean. For instance, we have this song:

> 'We are the Temple boys,
> We make a lot of noise.

We laugh and shout
Let our feelings out!
Oh, we are the Temple boys, Yeh!'

OK, maybe it doesn't look so great just set down on cold paper, but you should hear us when we go on the rampage through the outer courts when no one's there! The rabbis usually pretend not to notice — so long as we don't do it too often or when something important is going on. They realize we need to let off a bit of steam occasionally.

Anyway, as I said, I'm very happy there. Or I was, until one day I noticed something about the Law.

It always seemed to be saying, Don't do this or you'll get zapped. Obey this Law or you've got it coming to you. The only way out was by killing some poor innocent animal such as a dove or a lamb. That was the bit I hated. Oh, it made you think about not doing things wrong, so you wouldn't have to see an animal suffer, but it didn't really stop you. This bothered me a lot. In fact it kept going round and round in my head until I just had to get away from the place. So for the first time in my life I played hookey.

I've got this uncle, see, Uncle Andrew, who takes a bit of an interest in me. He often comes by the Temple to tell me what he's up to. Anyway, this day he came by and told me he was going up to Galilee. It's a few days' journey there and the same back, of course, and he'd be staying with some friends for a couple of nights.

I'd had a lot of exams lately and we'd been told we could ease off a bit, so I asked him if I could go with him. He asked if my teachers would mind, but I told him about the exams being over and so on. Anyway, he believed me, so I grabbed some clean clothes and shot off before anyone could stop me.

We talked a lot on the way up. It's not all that far, but it's really weird what happens to the climate as you go. It's scorchingly hot along the Jordan valley, but it's not a good idea for a devout Jew to go the other way, through the cooler hills of Samaria, so we had no choice. But at least the heat there is dry. The nearer you get to Galilee the hotter and — well, *soggier* it gets, till it sort of wraps itself round you like a hot, damp blanket, and by the time you get there you feel as if you're suffocating. It takes a day or two to get used to the change.

The River Jordan isn't as big as people think. I mean, people who've never seen it. But after the spring rains it can be quite impressive. All along the banks it's so green — trees, date palms, reeds. It makes a wonderful change from the dusty Jerusalem streets.

We often took a break and swam in the Jordan, but I was looking forward to reaching the Sea of Galilee so that I could swim for miles and miles if I wanted. I fancied doing a spot of fishing too. I hadn't realized how much I needed to get away from the Temple until we reached the river. Then I didn't know how I'd stuck it so long without breaking loose.

I told Uncle Andrew about those rules going round and round in my head, and about the sacrifices and so on, and he said, 'That's because there's a dimension — a depth — to the Law which isn't always mentioned.'

'What's that?' I asked.

'Well,' he said slowly, 'the laws aren't there to hem us in. The real laws of God are there to keep us safe.'

I'd never heard or thought of it like that before, so I asked him what he meant.

'It's not easy to explain', he said. 'I'll introduce you to someone who can do it better than I can.'

Another funny thing about going to Galilee is that as you go down that last hill to the sea — it's a pretty steep drop — you go deaf. Well, *I* did. I didn't stay deaf, but it took a couple of hours before my ears popped and I could hear properly again. It's to do with losing so much height so quickly, Uncle Andrew said. Maybe I shouldn't have run so fast! It didn't bother him, trudging along behind, but I found it really weird. What with the wet heat and the deafness, as soon as we got there I found a corner and curled up for the rest of the afternoon.

It wasn't until next day that I met the friend Uncle Andrew said could explain this business about the Law and the extra — what was it? — oh, yes, *dimension*.

Uncle Andrew came round to the fisherman's cottage where he'd found me a bed, and we made our way up the side of the hill sloping up from the sea. I'd caught a glimpse of the sea as we'd topped that last hill the day before, and I'd never seen anything so beautiful. Not even the Temple with all its gold and so on. It was so blue and calm, and so — quiet. This morning, as we made our way up the hill, I'd much rather have gone *down*hill for a swim than listened to another teacher, even if he was different, as Uncle Andrew promised.

Anyway, he also promised me a swim later, so up we climbed. There were lots of people sitting down in a huge semicircle, all looking up towards a higher point where a man was standing. He seemed to be unaware of the crowds, despite the noise they were making. In fact he was standing there with his back to them, looking upward with his arms stretched downward as if he were talking to someone. Uncle Andrew greeted a few of his friends, then we found a rock to sit on as near to the rabbi as we could. Well, Uncle Andrew called him Rabbi, but he didn't look much like one to me. For a start he was dressed in ordinary clothes, nothing fancy, but who was I to argue?

Because of this, I was looking at him quite closely, and it was amazing. When he stopped looking up and turned to the crowd, the noise stopped as if someone had cut it off with a knife! And everyone settled down and looked at him as if they expected him to really come up with the goods.

And he did. I'll never forget what he said. It wasn't just the setting — the sunshine, the sea, and the quiet. It was what he said.

I'm trained to take what a rabbi says and put it in my own

words. That way I can be sure I understand it and can pass it on when I get to be a rabbi. Here's some of it in a nutshell:

'You'll be happy if you are gentle because God will give you a beautiful new world to enjoy.*

'You'll be happy if you show mercy because God will show you mercy when you need it.

'You'll be happy if you keep your heart pure because that's the only way you'll ever see the purity of God.

'You'll be happy if you try to make peace because you will be called a child of God.'

So far so good. But then he had me sitting up, all ears.

'Unless you are better than the Scribes and Pharisees you will not get to heaven.'

That was a show-stopper, that one. They are the top dogs in the Temple. No one, but no one, can be better than the Scribes and Pharisees! They know every single law and they don't break any! I was about to say something to Uncle Andrew but he shook his head.

'Listen', he said. So I listened.

'You know you shouldn't kill. Fine. But it's just as bad to hate someone. God can't accept your love to *him* if you hate your brother.'

'If you think about doing something wrong for long enough you will do it. So don't let your mind stay on bad things.

'You've heard it said that if someone blinds you it's all right to blind them in return. If he knocks out a tooth, you can knock out his tooth. But you mustn't even *think* about getting your own back. Or where will it end? It's not enough to love just your friends. The best way to get rid of an enemy is to make him your friend. You can't do that if you're knocking his teeth out!

'You are all God's children. He forgives you if you do wrong. Therefore you have to forgive your brother if he hurts you. If you don't, God will not forgive you, and it's a terrible thing not to be forgiven by God.

'Try to live close to God, and he will help you to behave towards other people the way you want them to behave towards you.

'Ask for God's help and he will give it.

'Look for his guidance and he will lead you.'

I'll be quite honest now. I had never heard anyone talking like that before in my life! He made it sound so simple. The rabbis — well, once they got going you wondered how you'd ever remember all the laws, never mind *keep* them! It was as if a great load had been lifted off my mind. Instead of those laws chasing each other round and round, it all seemed to boil down to: Love God and other people. In fact, that's what this Rabbi said.

'But, Uncle Andrew', I said when the rabbi stopped speaking. 'How can it be that simple? What about the laws?'

'They're only guidelines, Theo,' he explained. 'They're there to protect us, not get us into trouble with God. If we love God we can't help loving each other.

'Can't you see, it's love that makes the rules work! Without love we can't do anything. And God can give us all the love we need. We only have to ask.'

When I got back to the Temple a week later I knew I was in *big* trouble. They hadn't given me permission to go, and the rules were very strict. At least they hadn't been looking for me because I'd left a quick note when I'd grabbed my clothes, but it didn't make much difference. The punishments for breaking the rules were quite severe, so I did my best to smooth things over. I tried to tell them about love making the rules work — and I put in a heavy bit about mercy. (I figured I needed all I could get!) That didn't help either. I copped it anyhow.

But I'm going to see Uncle Andrew. I can't stay in the Temple now. Life has *got* to be more than following a set of rules.

I just know that what Jesus said on that hillside by the sea is right. He made me feel nearer to God in five minutes than I've ever done in all my years as a Temple boy.

---

* See Matthew chapters 5, 6, 7.

SERVANT GIRL (1)

by Ruth

It's hard to believe we worried how I'd get on having to serve two mistresses — especially sisters! But they really are the kindest people, my ladies and their brother Lazarus. I've never had a minute's bother and I've made enough mistakes to drive the average person crazy!

It also seems hard to believe I've been here in Bethany for over a month. I know it's that long because Mum came over with presents for my birthday yesterday. It was clever of her to make twelve different little cakes, one for each year. Not that she needs to worry about me not getting enough to eat. I just about live in the kitchen, and the family do a lot of entertaining.

The kitchen's a lovely room, all bright and cool. That's because it's got two windows, and except on the hottest days, you can usually feel a slight breeze. The larger window at the back looks out over the courtyard. There's a grapevine growing along wires strung across, and the big leaves make it all shady and cool. But unlike most courtyards, ours is open at the back with this fantastic view of the hills of Judea. You can see people coming when they're miles away.

That was one of my jobs (on the day I want to tell you about) — to keep an eye on the road and let my ladies know when the Preacher and his friends were in sight. How I was supposed to do that when we were trying to get everything ready for all those hungry men I don't know. But let me tell you about my ladies first.

There's Martha. She doesn't make me call her ma'am or anything fancy, just Martha. She's always on the go. She loves having people in for meals, but then gets into a real tizwoz trying out new dishes she's afraid won't come off. By the time the guests arrive she's usually a nervous wreck. And she has indigestion for days after! But she can be so funny, always laughing and shouting about the place.

Mary's the opposite — in some ways. She's jolly too, but much quieter. Where Martha would rush in, lay the table in five minutes and have to rush back several times with things she's forgotten, Mary takes ages, placing each plate or dish exactly so, arranging flowers in a little pot, and then going off into a daydream and just gazing out of the window towards the hills. She spends a lot of time doing that, as if there's someone she's expecting and can't wait for them to arrive.

She was like that the day Jesus (the Preacher) and his friends came.

At first we were all busy in the kitchen. Then Martha asked Mary to see to the water for the men when they came in. We didn't see much of her after that. I offered to help with the big stone jar but she said she could manage so we left her to it. We were busy baking some new cakes and Martha wasn't sure if they'd turn out right. She was just putting them in the oven when Mary came in from the other room.

'They've just come over the hill!'

She looked so excited as she started to get the drinks ready, and it wasn't long before we could hear their voices as they entered the courtyard. I was standing at the sink and saw the Preacher as he came in. He looked very hot and tired but when Mary came outside he held out his arms and gave her a big hug. Martha left the cakes for a second and gave him a wave through the kitchen window. He waved back, still hugging Mary, then they all went in.

While the men were washing their feet Mary came into the kitchen, partly to give them privacy but also to finish the drinks.

'Martha!' she said, when she saw Martha was still baking. 'What are you doing? They're here!'

Martha didn't say much, just looked a bit cross and muttered to herself. Mary took the drinks out and that was the last we saw of her again until Martha sent me into the room for the empty glasses. As I went in Jesus was talking to Mary. She was sitting on the floor at his feet (well, there wasn't room anywhere else), and she was hanging on to every word he said. He smiled at me as I picked up his glass and Mary asked me to fill them again.

When I got back to the kitchen Martha was really cross.

'Why didn't she do the drinks herself? She knows I need you in here. Oh, well, do it quickly and get back as soon as you can.'

I did as she told me and took the big jug into the other room. Mary was still sitting on the floor and Jesus wasn't looking quite so hot and tired as he had when he came in. I had just finished refilling the men's glasses when Martha burst into the room.

'Lord,' she said, 'don't you mind that my sister has left me to prepare the food alone? Tell her to come and help me!'*

I was just thinking, what about *me* — *I'm* helping — when Jesus replied.

'Martha, Martha,' he said gently, 'you're trying to provide too much. Mary has got it right. It's *you* we want to see, not many dishes. Only one thing is important, to learn the will of God as Mary has chosen to do.'

Martha looked a bit embarrassed then, but Jesus smiled at her in such a lovely, understanding way that she couldn't help smiling back at him. He stood up then and went across and gave her a big hug just as he had Mary. Then she remembered the meal and wriggled free.

'The cakes!' she squealed, and shot out of the room. One 57

thing I did notice, though. For the rest of his visit there was a lot less to do in the kitchen, and Jesus had to make room for both of them at his feet!

Something else even more wonderful happened. He invited me to join them! It didn't matter that I'm only a servant. He treats everyone as if they were the *only* one.

And he talks about God all the time. But it's different from the men in the synagogue. He makes it sound as if God is his Father — I mean his own, personal Father.

After he'd gone I heard Lazarus and his sisters talking. They really believe that he is God's son — the Messiah they called him. And he's so kind, and good, and gentle, and full of life, and we were all so happy while he was here, that I'm beginning to think they're right.

I'm a bit like Mary nowadays, for ever looking out of the window, hoping to see the Preacher striding over the hill towards our house. I want to tell him how much we miss him when he's not here. Ask him to tell us more about his Father. Tell him I've decided to be one of his followers too.

---

* See Luke 10:38-42.

SERVANT GIRL (2)

by Ruth

Terrible deeds have been done here in Jerusalem.

You remember all the lovely things I told you about the Preacher, Jesus? Well the Romans have crucified him!

Even as I write it's hard to believe, but I know it's true because I saw him carrying a cross through the streets, with people jeering and shouting, and the Roman guards lashing him on. It was the most awful thing I've ever seen. They'd half killed him already. And I don't know what he'd done to deserve it, though I think it may have been our fault. You see, we welcomed him back to Jerusalem as if he were a king.

I don't think I can live with it if it really was our fault. He was so *good*. He didn't deserve to die. I can't tell you how empty everything seems, knowing we'll never see him coming over the hill again. And it was so lovely the day we made him king.

It was the first day of the week. We were with crowds of people on the road to Jerusalem to celebrate the Passover. Suddenly the crowd parted and there was Jesus — riding on a donkey. Everyone started grabbing palm branches from the trees and laying them in his path. I nearly rushed over to talk to him, but he looked so — I don't know — a bit pale and stern, and so — so, *kingly* is the only word I can think of. But I wanted him to see how glad I was that he was back, so I took my new scarf off and threw it on the ground in front of the donkey because I thought he'd notice the bright red and look at me. Lots of other people started throwing coats and scarves down then, and people were shouting 'Hosanna! Blessed is the king that comes in the name of the Lord!'*

I picked my scarf up again afterwards, but can't bear to wash out the dusty hoofprints because it was only a few days later that they turned against him.

It was the priests and Pharisees. They made the people believe he was bad, and they had him arrested in a garden on the Mount of Olives. The next morning they took him to the Romans and had him charged with treason. That's why I think it was our fault, treating him like a king. The Romans won't accept anyone as king except Caesar.

It was terrible. They wouldn't even let Pilate release him for Passover, and they shouted awful things and told Pilate to crucify him. I heard about it when I took a message into the city. Everyone was talking about it. Suddenly I couldn't take any more and ran all the way home, crying. But when I got there no one was in. A note from Martha said to stay indoors — they'd gone into the city to see if they could help Jesus. I didn't know how long they'd been gone but I decided to go back and try to find them, though I didn't have much hope with all those crowds.

In the end I decided anything was better than just sitting there crying and not knowing, so I set off back to the city. I knew where the crowd had been heading. There's only one place they crucify people. I made my way to Skull Hill.

It was worse than I'd imagined. The streets were full of people, many weeping — and not just the women.

'He saved my boy,' one woman cried.

'He gave me back my sight,' a man shouted.

Other people asked, 'What are they killing him for? What did he *do*?'

That's when I saw Jesus stumbling along with that great heavy cross. He looked half dead and I couldn't bear to look.

Suddenly I felt a hand on my shoulder and one of Jesus's

friends said, 'Go home, Ruthy. There's nothing you can do. This is no place for a child.'

'I want to tell him I'm sorry,' I cried, but he shook his head.

'It's not your fault. Do as you're told. Go back to the house.'

He looked so upset that it made me even more frightened than I had been so I did as I was told. When the others came home hours later my ladies were weeping so much they could hardly speak.

As I took their cloaks (wet from a heavy storm about three o'clock) Mary suddenly burst out:

'He forgave them, Ruth, even as they were hammering in the — the nails!' She broke down, then pulled herself together. 'And then — in all his pain and torment — he remembered his mother and — and asked John to look after her.'

'It was dark,' she said in a more controlled voice. 'for hours. While he hung there . . . '

Martha sank wearily onto the bench inside the door. 'How could it end like this, after all he's done — all our hopes?'

The Sabbath day had begun by then, and I hope never to see a sadder one as long as I live.

Joseph of Arimathea had offered his own tomb as a last resting place for the Master, but there hadn't been time before the Sabbath came in to anoint his body. So, early on the next day (the first day of the week) the women went to the tomb with spices long before I was up.

When they returned, hours later, their story was almost unbelievable.

Although Jesus had told his closest friends he would have to die but that he'd rise again on the third day, I don't think they believed him. But the Roman authorities, when they heard about it, had thought it worth putting a guard on the tomb. Not because they thought he'd rise, but to make sure his friends didn't steal his body and pretend he'd risen.

As Mary, with the mother of James, and Salome, went to the tomb in the first light of dawn, they wondered how to move the stone from the entrance. They knew all the men were still in hiding, but when they got there the huge stone had already been rolled away. They were a bit puzzled, and went up to the grave to see what was going on.

They got the fright of their lives. The grave clothes they'd wrapped Jesus's body in on Friday were lying there empty, and a young man they'd never seen before was sitting on the right side. He was dressed in a long white robe, and he nearly scared them to death.

When he saw them he stood up and said, 'Don't be afraid. You are looking for Jesus of Nazareth, who was crucified. He is not here, for he is risen. Look, this is where they laid him.'

Mary and the others just stared at the grave clothes while the young man went on: 'Go and tell his followers — and Peter — that he has gone to Galilee. You'll find him there, just as he told you.'

With that the women rushed back into the city and Mary went to tell Peter and the others, but *they didn't believe her!* It got them moving, though, and Peter and Mark ran to the grave and saw for themselves. Mary had followed them and when they left the grave she couldn't take in what had happened and was standing there, weeping, when a man spoke to her.

'Woman,' he said, 'why are you weeping?'

Mary thought it was a gardener and so she replied, 'Because they've taken away my Lord and I don't know where they've put him.'

Then the man said, 'Mary,' and suddenly Mary realized it was Jesus himself. She couldn't believe it, though, and reached out to touch him to make sure she wasn't dreaming, but he told her not to because he hadn't yet seen his Father. Then he told her to go and tell everyone.

She told us his exact words: 'Tell my brothers I'm going to my Father, and your Father, to my God and your God.'

We arrived in Capernaum yesterday evening, to see Peter, but he wasn't there. We met some friends of his who said he'd gone fishing. So, early this morning, when they'd be bringing in the catch, we went down to the lake. We saw the boat pulled up on the shore, and the men hauling in the nets. It must have been a good night for fishing because they could hardly manage the massive catch.

As we walked along the shore towards them, we saw that a man had got a fire going and was already cooking some fish on it. We heard him call to Peter and the others.

'Bring some more fish!' he called, holding up a bread cake. 'You'll be needing breakfast.'

They finished stacking the last of the fish boxes, then went across to the stranger, looking a bit puzzled and hesitant. We followed, and as we got nearer I was almost sure it was Jesus. But it couldn't be. My eyes had to be playing tricks. Jesus was dead. The Romans had made very sure of that! Anything I felt to the contrary was just wishful thinking.

But then, as we all settled down round him, the man turned and broke the bread. Suddenly no one had any doubts — it *was* Jesus! We'd seen those beautiful hands too often, measuring out blessings and bread.

We took the bread and fish and ate as if in a dream. No one could bring themselves to say anything. We daren't do or say anything which might wake us up! We were just so happy to be with him again.

After a while Jesus took Peter aside and they walked along the shore together. They talked for a long time, and three times I saw Jesus ask Peter something. Each time he spoke he stopped walking as if what he was asking was very important. And each time Peter seemed to be trying to convince him of something.

Eventually they came back along the shore. We finished breakfast together then, and I watched as Jesus ate some fish, which proved he was no ghost!

I can't begin to describe the change that has come over us all since we saw Jesus again. All during that awful Sabbath when he lay resting in the tomb our hopes, our minds, our joy, even our bodies, felt totally crushed. There had seemed to be no meaning to anything any more.

Then he was among us again, and it meant so much more than someone having been brought back to life only to die again — like my master Lazarus.

In rising from the tomb Jesus has conquered death itself. He has opened a door for all who believe in him. A door that leads to eternal life. A door that leads back to his Father — *our* Father.

A little while after that wonderful breakfast on the beach at Galilee, Jesus returned to Jerusalem, where he gave us a special commission: 'Go into all the world and preach the good news to all creation.'

Then, after leading us to Bethany he lifted his hands in a final blessing, and was taken up into heaven.

It was a long time before we could tear our eyes from the burning blue sky, but it was no tearful farewell this time. Before he left, Jesus promised he will come again, and when he does we will be with him and the Father for ever.

Our joy is complete.

---

*See Mark 11, then Matthew 27, John 19, 20 and 21, and Luke 23 and 24 for the full story.